The ESP Marriage

Develop True Intimacy in Your Marriage by Building a Powerful EMOTIONAL, SPIRITUAL, and PHYSICAL Connection

Nashawn Turner

Copyright © 2008 by Nashawn Turner

The ESP Marriage
Develop True Intimacy in Your Marriage by Building a Powerful EMOTIONAL, SPIRITUAL, and PHYSICAL Connection
by Nashawn Turner

Printed in the United States of America

ISBN 978-1-60647-389-4

All rights reserved solely by the author. The author guarantees all contents are original and do not infringe upon the legal rights of any other person or work. No part of this book may be reproduced in any form without the permission of the author. The views expressed in this book are not necessarily those of the publisher.

Unless otherwise indicated, Bible quotations are taken from The New King James Version of the Spirit-Filled Life Bible. Copyright © 1991 by Thomas Nelson, Inc.

www.xulonpress.com

DEDICATION

This book is dedicated to couples everywhere who desire to know and experience true intimacy in their marriages.

TABLE OF CONTENTS

Acknowledgements ix
Foreword xiii
Introduction xvii
How to use the book xix
Chapter 1: What is Intimacy? 21
Chapter 2: The Need for Intimacy 29
Chapter 3: Myths about Intimacy 37
Chapter 4: Does Your Marriage Have ESP? 45
Chapter 5: The "E" Factor – Emotional Intimacy 49
Chapter 6: The "S" Factor – Spiritual Intimacy 57
Chapter 7: The "P" Factor – Physical Intimacy 65
Chapter 8: Growing in ESP for a Lifetime of Intimacy 77
Afterword 87
Recommended Reading and Resources 89
Biography of Author 93

ACKNOWLEDGEMENT

First, I like to thank God for this wonderful opportunity to write this book and to share the enormous gratitude I have for all that He has done in my life and marriage. Your blessings overwhelm me and your love truly amazes me. Thank you God for your faithfulness in granting me the fulfillment of a promise and a dream come true.

I also want to thank God for the good and perfect gift that He has given to me in my husband, Keith. Truly, I have had the wonderful privilege of living, loving, and enjoying the ESP concept intimately with you for 19 years of marriage. It has been an awesome journey!

In addition to my husbands' love and support, I like to thank my three incredible children, Tayler, Mikaela, and Nathan for trying to be patient when mommy was writing this book and clapping and shouting thunderously when it was over. There is nothing like having my own cheerleading squad! You all are my greatest gifts! Know that you all are my heart and soul and I am honored to be your mother. I love you always!

Next, I would like to thank my family who has shared in my excitement, as this book project became a reality. However, a special thanks goes out to my mom, Lillie Harmon for being a wonderful mother. She once told me that Keith would one day be my husband. Well, mom you were right! Thank you for giving us your blessing from the beginning.

I also would like to thank my mother and father-in-law, Wendell and Gloria Turner who welcomed me into their family with much love and laughter. You two have been a great role model for marriage and that example has given us something to look forward to in our own marriage! I could not have been more blessed nor could I have asked for a better family to be apart of. Thanks for being such great in-laws!

Next, I owe a tremendous amount of thanks to my book coach and accomplished author, Monique Brown McKenzie. It was because of her that this book even came into existence. From the moment she attended my Let's talk about Intimacy and Sex...Does your Marriage have ESP? Workshop, she shared with me how this whole concept screams "book"!!! She so graciously offered to work with me in order to transpose the workshop into a book. Monique's professional assistance, support, and feedback helped me make it possible for more marriages to have access to practical and powerful tools to transform their marriages. It's been a pleasure working with you...you are the best!

Furthermore, I would like to thank my best friend Joy Williams for walking along side of me with her continuous prayers, her words of encouragement, her laughter, and her resourceful eye. (Thanks for the wonderful suggestions that helped me to write my last chapter – it's a perfect ending). Joy, your friendship has been like none other throughout the years and I appreciate it more than you know. As I have embarked on this journey of writing my first book, you continue to celebrate and believe in all that God has put in me to bless other marriages. Thank you for being a true friend.

Of course, I would be remiss if I did not thank my fellow Mocha Mom and friend, Lorraine Morris-Cole. Lorraine you are one of the most giving and creative persons that I have met in a long time. Thank you for sharing with me your knowledge, wisdom, ideas, and advice as I was writing this book. I am truly grateful to you for freely investing in something that is so dear to my heart.

I also have to thank Dr. Jeff Gardere for his powerful endorsement of my book. What an awesome masterpiece you are to the work of empowering marriages and relationships. Thank you for offering your gift of words that echo volumes regarding what ***The ESP Marriage*** book represents.

Last, but not least I want to thank all of my friends who believed that a book about marriage was in me all along and who have waited with great anticipation for its arrival. Many of you saw the vision unfold and was delighted to support me with your love and faith. I celebrate each and every one of you.

With Much Love,

Nashawn

FOREWORD

I have had the wonderful pleasure of knowing Nashawn Turner for nearly 20 years. When we met, we were both newlyweds, green with excitement about life and love. Her passion for purpose and fulfillment in her own life is contagious as she motivates and encourages others to do the same. Because of our friendship, I have had the unique privilege of seeing Nashawn and her husband, Keith, interact over the years. They display the many joys and challenges of marriage with the up most respect and dignity for each other and the life they share. As a result, I was particularly thrilled when I learned of this workbook, literally birthed from her very powerful "Does Your Marriage Have ESP?" workshop series – a series that continues to touch and transform countless marriages.

The ESP marriage is a thought-provoking approach to examining the quality and potential in the marital relationship. This adventure into intimacy will interest and excite both husbands and wives seeking to communicate their heart to their spouse. By exploring emotional, physical and spiritual intimacy (ESP), Nashawn provides a fresh and insightful view on marriage and the factors contributing to fulfillment for both men and women.

As I survey my own marriage of twenty plus years, the factors affecting intimacy remain an endless journey of twist and turns. The ESP marriage helps to unravel the often complicated issues revolving around our common desire to know and be known. By uniquely giving voice to both spouses, it is a multidimensional approach to discovering, communicating and celebrating the oneness of the marriage covenant. Wherever you are on the spectrum of marital health, drowning in conflict or enjoying a fun-filled cruise, the ESP marriage can help you identify the areas in your marriage requiring the greatest attention. Having assessed the need, you are also given tools to commit to getting your marriage afloat or keeping it going full steam ahead.

Even with the many obstacles and distractions of our ultramodern lifestyles, this workbook demonstrates that emotional, spiritual and physical intimacy is indeed possible. Delivered with a straightforward approach and real life examples, newlyweds and seasoned marriages alike will benefit from the content found in these pages. Nashawn encourages us to embrace marriage as a commitment of our total selves being joined with the one we have promised to have and to hold. Whatever you have or desire to hold onto, your life and love will surely be enhanced as you embark on building an ESP marriage.

Joy A. Williams
Author of Friendship MAPS: Heart Connections for Life's Journey

PRAISES FOR the *"Let's Talk Intimacy and Sex...Does Your Marriage Have ESP?"* Workshop has now become *"THE ESP MARRIAGE" BOOK!*

The "Let's talk intimacy and sex...Does your marriage have ESP?" workshop was very informative and I thoroughly enjoyed it! It wasn't just about sex, but more about intimacy and oneness in a marriage. **-C. Campbell, Marrietta, GA**

The "Let's talk intimacy and sex ... Does your marriage have ESP?""was a great workshop. It taught me how to reconnect and have a deeper understanding of my husband's needs. Too bad it could not have been longer. Nashawn was phenomenal!!! And her energy was great!- **S. Fitzpatrick, Atlanta, GA**

Nashawn was great and very personable!!! The information from the "intimacy and sex" workshop was valuable"information on ways to spice up your marriage!"- **R. Ausbrey**

Nashawn was very real and personable! The Let's talk intimacy and sex" workshop helped me to understand how to please our husbands and ourselves. Thanks you for your service in saving marriages. Love the gifts and ideas!! **- T. Price, Washington, DC**

At the Let's talk about intimacy and sex...Does your marriage have ESP?" workshop, I learned to be more in tune with my spouse. I liked that Nashawn told us that no two marriages are the same. Nashawn was awesome because she kept it real!!!"- **L. Crockett, Odenton, MD**

"Let's talk intimacy and sex...Does your marriage have ESP?" workshop I learned about loving yourself and allowing yourself to love your man emotionally, spiritually, and physically. I wanted to hear more of Nashawn! She was awesome! Real with Purpose!!
- S. Butler, Memphis, TN

The marriage seminar was great, honest and funny! **-Anonymous**

The intimacy workshop is great for old couples and new couples!!! Helpful tips and discussion! **- G. Redd**

The seminar on intimacy helped me to learn ways to think outside the box. More women need to know that it's not all about them, but it's about our choices.- **T. Robinson**

At Nashawn's workshop, I learned about what most won't discuss. This is a very important topic for married couples. **- M. Robertson**

I believe the "Let's talk intimacy and sex...Does your marriage have ESP?" workshop could help every marriage. Nashawn did a great job!!! I wish more time could have been added." - **C. Artis**

INTRODUCTION

When I first created the *Let's Talk about Intimacy and Sex... Does Your Marriage Have ESP?* workshop for a conference about two years ago, I had no idea of the response that I would get from it. Since doing this particular session, it has become one of the most popular ones that I have ever facilitated. Still, I never envisioned that this concept would ever evolve into a book.

Women, especially, have told me how much this workshop has changed their marriages. They found that the workshop has refreshed, inspired, and motivated them to invest in every area of their marriage so they can get the best out of it. Once the women left the workshop, they were excited to see their husbands and to put the things they'd learned into practice. Many who attended the workshop found that the "ESP" keys were the missing ingredients to their marriages and that after implementing them; their marriages were much improved. Even husbands agreed that the information that their wives learned at the workshop was instrumental in redesigning their marriages.

The reality is that many married couples are in search of the missing ingredient. Some think that the missing ingredient is a new spouse. I strongly disagree with this type of thinking. What I am talking about is something much deeper. I'm talking about the heart and soul of a marriage—Intimacy. I believe that the greater the intimacy, the greater the marriage. Yet, discovering how to develop

The ESP Marriage

great intimacy is a journey that rewards with incredible fulfillment and satisfaction for a strong marriage.

The development of strong intimate marriages includes the three major building blocks or keys of "ESP". The Emotional, Spiritual, Physical elements are the keys that will unlock the hidden treasures and explore the depth of marital happiness and security for an awesome future together. So I invite you to find out if your marriage has ESP and use the information in this interactive guide to help you improve the level of intimacy between you and your spouse.

HOW TO USE THIS BOOK

Dear Reader,

The purpose of this book is to help married couples discover how to transform their marriage with the three most powerful keys for developing true intimacy.

I hope this book inspires couples to transcend their current level of intimacy while motivating them to reach beyond what is, to embrace what could be the most enriching experience shared between two people.

This interactive guide is designed to lead couples in a step-by-step process of exploring the emotional, spiritual and physical components of their marriage by reading about everyday life experiences that occur in marriages. Each life scenario corresponds with thought provoking questions that will enable couples to gain insight and understanding regarding their own ESP needs while learning how to effectively meet those specific needs using the ESP concepts.

The **"Jump Start Action Plan"** was created to help couples set intimacy goals and to assist them in moving forward with action for implementing change.

The **"Key Points to Remember"** offers a quick synopsis of the main points covered in each section of the book. The Key Points reminds couples of the important concepts to focus on.

The **"ESP Tips"** empowers couples with life-changing wisdom that is useful in overcoming intimacy challenges.

Lastly, the **"Prayer"** section is to inspire and connect couples to God and His divine power to change the complexion of any marriage. Couples are to use the written prayers or they can make up their own prayers in order to invite God to intervene on their behalf. The Prayer portion will aid couples in strengthening their faith and trust in God, and it will deepen their spiritual relationship to each other. Prayer will produce change in the "inner life" of the relationship and it will ultimately influence the couple's perspective regarding their entire emotional, spiritual, and physical intimacy experience.

I once heard T. D. Jakes make a powerful statement while preaching to his church about change. The statement was *"It will work, if you work it"*. When T. D. Jakes made this statement, he was preaching about applying effort to overcome life's issues and create change. However, I believe that the same rule applies to marriage. If you decide to become fully engaged in your marriage, this workbook will work for you if you work it. You will learn all about ESP, gain intimate knowledge of your own marriage so that you and your spouse can grow into a stronger couple, and experience a long lasting emotional, spiritual, and physical closeness. Get ready because your best marriage awaits you!

Happy Reading!

CHAPTER ONE

What Is Intimacy?

"Adam knew, loved and had intimate knowledge of Eve's spirit and soul before he ever became intimate with her body" ~ Bob Yandian~ Author of ***One Flesh***

A while ago, I received a phone call from a friend of mine who wanted advice about how to help her friend who has been having some serious marital problems for quite some time. She shared with me that her friend has been cheating on her husband and was looking for someone to help her to justify within her own mind why this was ok. According to the friend, her husband just doesn't pay attention to her anymore.

She stated that when he comes home from work, he is always tired. All he wants to do is eat dinner, look at television, and then go to bed. She feels as if he tries to avoid her as much as possible and when she tries to be intimate with him, he becomes rude and insulting. She says it has been a long time since they spent any real quality time together. In fact, she said that things are so bad in their marriage that they barely talk to each other. The lack of intimacy was so apparent that her husband prefers to communicate by text messaging than to speak face-to-face with his wife.

After many attempts to try to reconnect with her husband, the wife remained frustrated. She missed being the "apple of his eye". She missed his tender words of love towards her and about her. She missed the quality time that they used to share on quiet evenings. She missed the times they shared what was going on in each other's lives as each listened with deep interest and care.

More than anything, she longed for the spiritual closeness they shared. She thought about the many times when problems arose, that they would surrender every issue to God for wisdom on how to handle it and bring closure. She also yearned for the physical closeness they both looked so forward to that completed their union. Now there seems to be nothing but pain, anger and frustration between her and her spouse. But with the new fling, things were very different. When "he" came along, he was able to heal all of her hurts after one encounter together.

After hearing this story, I often wondered what happened to this couple? What lead them to this place of acting cold and unresponsive to one another? What was in the making before the wife decided to step out on her marriage vows to engage in an extramarital affair? Where did the intimacy go in this marriage? I also wondered if they ever had a deep intimate relationship with one another in the beginning.

You see, intimacy speaks a language all of its own. In order to hear the voice of intimacy and to relate to it, it requires vulnerability and trust from ones own heart, soul, and mind. I believe there is no quick fix for this marriage. But, the good news is, if this couple is willing to work things out by first acknowledging that they really do have a problem and are prepared to roll up their sleeves and do the necessary work, then intimacy can be restored.

But even if intimacy never existed for this couple, they can create it by investing the time and energy it takes for them to experience a fresh and new way to communicate their needs, desires, and wants for a fulfilling and satisfying marriage.

What if their problem suggests that they don't know what intimacy is? At a previous engagement where I was the facilitator for a small women's gathering, I begin to talk of this subject. As I begin to share about intimacy, one of the women in the group looked very confused and she interjected many questions as I continued to speak. Her confusion came from the moment she heard me say the word "intimacy" which was interpreted in her mind as meaning "sex".

This encounter helped me to see and understand that the word sex and intimacy are synonymous for some people and very distinct to others.

Therefore, since intimacy can mean different things to different people, how would you define intimacy? What does intimacy mean to you?

_____
_____
_____
_____
_____
_____
_____
_____

Webster's dictionary defines *intimacy* as marked by a very close association or contact with someone else of a very personal or private nature. Intimacy often includes a warm friendship that develops through long associations.

Let's explore my definition of intimacy. **Intimacy is *nurturing each other in those places that no one else knows about. It is where deep sharing takes place between you and your spouse that allows you two to become transparent and vulnerable.***

For example, before my husband and I were married, there was one very painful thing that happened in my childhood that I had never told anyone at that time. I guess I had never truly felt safe enough to share the molestation that I experienced as a child until I married Keith. This was partly due to the shame that I often associated with it. This was not an easy task for me to do because I feared what he might think about me. Nevertheless, I decided that I needed to share this with him.

As I shared my experience, the memory of my violation overwhelmed me with emotions. I remember saying to Keith, "Now that I'm with you, no one will ever be able to hurt me like that again." At that moment, Keith looked straight into my eyes, gently wiped my tears away with his fingers, and just held me ever so close in quietness. He waited quietly with me in my pain and assured me with his love that I was safe. This sense of safety caused me to believe that no one would ever be able to hurt me like that again. Becoming transparent and vulnerable allowed a deep nurturing to take place at one of our most intimate moments connecting us by the soul.

When you read the definition of intimacy, what comes to your mind?

_____
_____
_____
_____
_____
_____
_____

Real intimacy is as authentic as the person who is giving it. You will know it when you experience it because it connects you to the soul of another individual. But coming to an understanding about what real intimacy is *can* be a challenge. It was certainly a process that my husband and I had to learn when we got married 19 years ago. Was it easy for me to share some of the things that happened in my past with him? Absolutely, not!!! Yes, we were able to talk and share our feelings and our thoughts about some things, yet there were some limitations and some apprehensions about us sharing our "real selves" for fear of judgment and rejection.

How long did our limitations and apprehensions last? Our limitations and apprehensions lasted for about the first two years of our marriage. What changed? We changed. As individuals, we became more comfortable with ourselves and as a married couple, we became more comfortable with one another. In addition, we also decided to rid ourselves of the pretense so that we could be who we really are.

Maybe there are some limitations or apprehensions in your marriage. Or, maybe there is a fear of being judged or rejected by your spouse. Whatever it is, it doesn't have to stay that way. Dare to be intimate! Go beyond what feels comfortable to truly know your spouse in those areas that may have been closed off. You may be afraid but decide to be up for the challenge. This is just the beginning of entering that exclusive place reserved for the two of you. The results may surprise you.

List three reasons why you think intimacy has been a challenge for your marriage.

_____
_____
_____
_____
_____
_____
_____
_____

So, what do you do when intimacy corners you? What does being cornered by intimacy looks like? For example, when you are faced with dealing with something in the marriage that causes you to feel unhappy, and your spouse ask you what is wrong, do you tell him/her the truth? Do you fend off intimacy by resisting its touch, its sound, and its raw closeness? Do you resist intimacy because it makes you feel exposed and uncomfortable? Or, do you welcome it as a work of the heart that resembles the work that God does in us as He is steadily drawing us to himself?

Jeremiah 31:3 says that with love and kindness He (God) has drawn you. True intimacy will draw you to itself. However, just like our relationship with the Lord requires us to do something to draw near to Him, He promises that he will draw near to us (James 4:8).

ESP TIP: Deal with your intimacy issues upfront by addressing each issue one by one. Remember, becoming intimately acquainted with one another may be challenging, but think about the level of intimacy your marriage may be missing by not seeking to overcome those challenges.

List three ideas on how you and your spouse can create lasting moments of intimacy.

_____
_____
_____
_____
_____
_____
_____

I heard someone say that the word "intimacy" means "Into-Me-You-See". This kind of intimacy takes real courage. What are you willing to let your spouse see in you? In other words, are you willing to let yourself be known from the very core of your being?

The truth is that some couples may be afraid to let there spouse see what's inside. The fear that couples have usually involves wondering about whatever the other person might see in them may cause the other person to no longer love and accept them.

What is it worth to you and your marriage to truly embrace being vulnerable and exposed in order for real intimacy to emerge?

_____
_____
_____
_____
_____
_____
_____

What are you willing to do this week in order for the "Into-Me-You-See" type of intimacy level to be experienced? Name three things.

    1.
    2.
    3.

A Jump Start Action Plan
**(Feel free to create more of your own action steps
to continue to enhance intimacy in your marriage)**

1. This week share something that you always wanted to share with your spouse.
2. Play the "20 questions" game to learn something new that you did not know about your spouse.
3. Make time for you both to share your day's events. Commit to listening to each other without interruption.
4. Share an activity together that both of you love to do.
5. Rediscover each other's passions.
6.
7.
8.
9.
10.

Key Points to Remember:

- Define intimacy as it relates to your marriage.
- Learn how to cultivate it by opening up yourself and inviting it in with no reservation. This positions you and your spouse to be in control of the height, breadth, width, and depth of your intimate relationship.
- Remember becoming intimately acquainted with one another may be challenging, but weigh the challenges that could occur by not pursuing intimacy to the fullest.

PRAYER

Lord, intimacy is what you desire for every married couple to experience from the beginning. Help us to know the kind of intimacy that you created for us to enjoy fully and generously with one another. Holy Spirit draw us deep into the wells of intimacy that we can drink freely and as often as we like until we are completely satisfied. In Jesus Name, Amen.

CHAPTER TWO

The Need for Intimacy

"Love is as strong as death...many waters cannot quench love, nor can the floods drown it." Song of Solomon 8:6b-7 (Holy Bible, New King James Version)

It seems that people are afraid to need one another. Everyone wants to declare their independence by proving their ability to "do" life on their own. I like what contributing authors Elisa Morgan and Carol Kuykendall wrote about intimacy in *The Complete Marriage Book*. In their article called *"Husband and Wife and Baby Makes Three"*, the authors shared their view on intimacy. They believe that "intimacy in marriage is about learning to need each other, communicating that need, and figuring out how to continue to be comfortable with that need."

Recently, I had a conversation with a married woman who is apparently frustrated in her marriage. During a moment of frustration towards her husband, she let him know that she does not *need* him and that she can take care of herself without him; nevertheless, she does *want* him and chooses to be with him. I am not sure how her husband must have felt when she shared her true feelings but I am sure it must have been a revelation. Marriage is not about how independent we can be in our relationships, but rather how interdependent we can be as a family unit.

I wonder is there a fear that we have in our marriages about being vulnerable enough to express our need for each other. For example, Kerry and Jeff have been married for eight years. All of the eight years that Kerry and Jeff have been married, Kerry has been a stay at home mom. She loves being at home, but often times feel unappreciated by her husband who seems not to acknowledge her contribution to the household.

In other words, she feels as if he takes her for granted. One night when Jeff came home from work, he began to comment about how the house was not cleaned to his standards, how he feels overwhelmed with the bills, and how things would be different if she did not just sit around the house all day but did something to make life easier for him. Kerry was stunned. Jeff left out of the house in anger shouting, "I can do bad all by myself."

When Jeff later returned, Kerry decided to give him a piece of her mind. When Kerry told Jeff how she needed to feel needed by him, he found himself listening for the first time. He confessed that his anger was not towards her but towards life itself. He realized that the pressures of life have numbed him to the needs of anyone else but his own. Once Jeff cooled off, he felt it was time for them to sit down and talked about what they both felt that they needed from each other.

As Jeff listened to Kerry, he admitted that his behavior contributed to her feeling as though she didn't matter. From this day forward, Jeff and Kerry decided to work things out and to be more mindful of what they say and do in response to each other.

The need for intimacy in our marriage relationships is vital. Everyone wants and need to feel validated by the person who matters most to them, their spouse. Statistics has it that fifty percent of all marriages fail, but is it possible that many of those marriages are failing due to the absence of intimacy in the home? Lack of intimacy leaves marriages with a deep sense of emptiness. Could it be that intimacy or the lack thereof is the culprit behind many couple's inability to stay connected? Or, perhaps it's our inability to prioritize life in a way that benefits the marriage towards keeping intimacy alive and well in the home.

We all know that life happens, but learning to manage life well will preserve marital intimacy and cause it to thrive. Making life work for your marriage takes creativity, perseverance, and determination. However, for every godly marriage to work, it is mandatory to include God in the process. God is love and since God is love, our greatest defense in fighting for our marriages is to choose to love through the good times and the bad because love wins.

ESP TIP: Validate your spouse's need for intimacy by being willing to do what is required and necessary to meet that need.

How do you to preserve intimacy in your marriage?
_____
_____
_____
_____
_____
_____
_____
_____

Most men and women view intimacy differently. But how can we appreciate the different perspectives when we don't understand what they are. Dr. Willard F. Harley Jr. author of *"His Needs, Her Needs"*, ranked and described the five top needs of husbands and the five top needs of wives.

The five top needs of husbands are:

1. Sex
2. Recreational companionship
3. An attractive spouse
4. Domestic support
5. Respect and admiration

The five top needs of wives are:

1. Affection
2. Conversation
3. Honesty and openness
4. Financial support
5. Family commitment

List your spouse's five top needs

1.
2.
3.
4.
5.

The bible says in Ephesians 5:33 says "let each other of you in particular so love his own wife as himself, and let the wife see that she respects her husband." The bible places a distinction on the different needs that each person requires. However, a major need for all men is to feel respected and for every woman is to feel loved.

What major need do you have right now?
_____
_____
_____
_____
_____
_____
_____
_____

Husbands: List what makes you feel respected by your wife.

1.
2.
3.

4.
5.

Wives: List what makes you feel loved by your husband.

1.
2.
3.
4.
5.

As a husband, what does your wife need to do to show you that she respects you? Describe how that would look lived out in your marriage?

_____
_____
_____
_____
_____
_____
_____
_____

As a wife, what does your husband need to do to show you that he loves you? Describe how that would look lived out in your relationship?

_____
_____
_____
_____
_____
_____
_____
_____

The ESP Marriage

Now that you know what each other need to feel the kind of intimacy that satisfies, what will you do this week towards meeting the need?

_____
_____
_____
_____
_____
_____
_____
_____

A Jump Start Action Plan:
(Feel free to create more of your own action steps to continue to enhance your marital intimacy)

1. Run her bath water/give him a massage
2. Share a day without complaining
3. Grant one another time to be alone
4. Support each other's dreams
5. Plan to laugh everyday together
6.
7.
8.
9.
10.

Extra Activity: Pick out an object or use one word that describes the intimacy level of your marriage and tell why you chose this word or object.

Key Points to Remember:

- There is a need for intimacy like never before because of our busy lives. Fight to stay connected.
- Don't be afraid to tell each other what you need and purpose to connect heart to heart for the survival of your marriage.
- Husbands and wives have different needs. Find out what your spouse's needs are and meet those needs. Understand that the most important need for a man is respect and the most important need for a wife is love.
- Keep God in the process of achieving intimacy in your marriage. God is love and love wins.

PRAYER

Lord, we know that your Word says in 1Corinthians 13:4-8 that love suffers long and is kind. It also says love does not envy; it does not parade itself, it is not puffed up and it does not behave rudely. Love does not seek its own and is not provoked. Love thinks no evil and does not rejoice in iniquity but rejoices in the truth. When we question whether or not we are acting in love towards each other, help us to substitute our names in place of the word "love" to perform a "love check-up" in our marriage.

Then empower us to make the appropriate changes necessary to get back on track with the pursuit of true intimacy. More than anything help us to remember that love bears all things, believes all things, hopes all things, and endures all things. Remind us to always trust the kind of love that will never fail…God's love. Your love enables us to push pass the excuses and pride so we will not forget why we got married in the first place which is to be happily married for a lifetime.

CHAPTER THREE

Myths about Intimacy

"And you shall know the truth, and the truth shall make you free" John 8:32 (Holy Bible, New King James Version)

Once upon a time, long, long time ago, there was a couple who loved each other very, very much. One day this couple decided to get married and dreamed of living happily ever after. For a while, this couple seemed inseparable. It seemed as if they did everything together and enjoyed each other's company tremendously. They enjoyed long walks in the park, going out to dinner and museums, reading poetry together and attending poetry jams, going out with family and friends, watching old movies, going to the beach, and surprising each other with sunrise breakfasts and romantic rendezvous. There was rarely a time when you'd see one without the other. Despite of their busy work schedules, the couple always made time for one another. Intimacy was a major priority for them.

However, after about three years, a change occurred in their marriage. This couple began to have some real problems connecting with one another. They began to spend less and less time together. The husband said it was because his schedule at work had changed, requiring him to work longer hours. Once the husband gets home, he shares that he feels too tired to do anything other than relax. Although the wife attempted to be understanding initially, she still felt they should be able to spend at least a couple of hours together on the weekends. When this didn't happen, she felt frustrated and neglected. The last few years were nothing like when the first got married, the couple concluded.

The couple began to question what happened to the intimacy that they once shared, and why it seems so hard to recreate the same type of intimacy they had known for so long? They missed those dreamy days and nights of looking into each other's eyes, enjoying stolen kisses, snuggling in bed while whispering those sweet nothings. They missed those everyday feelings of anticipation because they couldn't wait to see and be with one another. Although this was nothing like the honeymoon, this couple never thought that they would fine themselves in this place. What went wrong?

This couple reflected back on what they learned in their pre-marital counseling sessions as well as what they read in books about marriage. They also thought about what other married couples have shared with them regarding intimacy. The pre-marital counseling and the books did not tell them that it takes a consistent effort from both parties to keep the level of intimacy strong and vibrant. What this couple believed was that they would always experience "marital bliss" just because they loved each other and believed that things would just work itself out. Yet they never fully understood the ebbs and flows of marital intimacy and the constant investment they needed to make in order for their marriage to experience intimacy on an everyday basis. What a rude awakening?

Knowing the truth about intimacy is key to experiencing true intimacy. Don't believe the hype or the myths! Maintaining true intimacy takes a lot of work. Often couples come into a marriage with some kind of preconceived idea about what intimacy is. Some never truly investigated the truth about what it takes to have the kind of closeness that continues to enrich the marriage relationship for a lifelong journey.

There are many prevailing myths about intimacy that have invaded many marriages. These myths have led to many marital problems. Let's look at a few of the prevailing myths that I've heard over the years…

- Marriage creates instant intimacy
- Sex is the ultimate expression of intimacy in marriage
- Women want intimacy more than men
- Intimacy in marriage is not all that important. Only our marriage vows matter.
- Some spouses are just not intimate people
- What you don't know won't hurt you
- Marriage will be as romantic as when we were dating

I am sure that there are many other myths that you've heard over the years as well, but let's take a moment to deal with just a few of the myths mentioned above.

1. *Marriage creates instant intimacy* is void of the reality that all aspects of a marriage takes work and lots of it. Building closeness in any relationship takes time and marriage is definitely not an exception.

2. *Sex is the ultimate expression of intimacy in marriage.* This is a myth. There are many couples that have great sex but their marriages are dead and distant. If you don't have a real connection, the two of you are just going through a physical exercise.

3. *Women want intimacy more than men.* The truth is men and women crave intimacy but in different ways as revealed in Dr. Willard F. Harley Jr.'s book, *His Needs, Her Needs*.

4. *Intimacy in marriage is not all that important. Only our marriage vows matter.* The bible says in Ephesians 6:24-33 that the husbands are to love their wives as Christ loves the church and gave Himself for it. This means there is a constant giving and supplying of needs in a marriage. The wife is to see that she respects her husband and the husband is to see that he loves his wife. These two things indicate a constant response to meet one another's core needs.

5 *Some spouses are just not intimate people.* Being intimate with someone is a behavior that can be learned. Remember, being intimate with someone is a choice based on a desire to be intimate.

6. *What you don't know won't hurt you.* This myth was revealed in the Garden of Eden when Adam and Eve tried to hide the truth from God about their own sin. Each were an accomplice to committing the sin which caused a disconnect from the intimacy they once shared with each other and God. So come clean regarding the real issues of your marriage. Without doing so, what you don't know might hurt you more than the two of you could ever imagine.

7. *Marriage will always be as romantic as when they were dating.* This myth is sometimes the hardest to de-myth especially for women because most women have fallen in love with the fantasy of love. The lack of reality that real love takes work is what is lost. Romance should be integrated into the marriage, but it is not what the entire marriage is about.

ESP TIP: Examine your own myths about love, marriage, and intimacy. Develop a "reality-based" understanding about marriage that is established on what you know to be true and what works.

What do you believe about how intimacy is created in marriage?

_____
_____
_____
_____
_____
_____
_____
_____

Maybe you're wondering... how is intimacy created in a marriage and what does it take to have the kind of intimacy that unites couples as one? Is intimacy something that just happens? Are some couples more blessed or gifted to experience a unique intimacy in their marriage more than others?

Let's look at how one couple created intimacy in their marriage.

Mike and Lisa were the best of friends before they got married over ten years ago. They knew that developing a friendship was essential to their relationship because they valued getting to know one another as individuals. They believed that getting to know one another as friends first would allow them to share themselves and to be fully accepting of each other. When they became romantically involved, their level of intimacy that they had developed during their friendship established a degree of intimacy in their lives as a married couple.

As years passed, Mike and Lisa had to continue to work at maintaining a strong level of intimacy that would sustain them in the good times and the bad times. They relied on the fact that they could depend on their friendship to weather the storm and overcome any obstacle together even when they did not feel all the warm fuzzies on the inside towards each other. For example, when Mike made an investment in the stock market from the money that he and Lisa had been saving for their dream home, things did not turn out as he had hoped. Mike thought by investing this money in the stock market would give them a greater return on their money to buy their dream home in a shorter time-frame then they had planned.

The bad thing about this is that not only did Mike lose the money, but he pursued the financial investment without consulting with Lisa first. His reasoning behind not consulting with Lisa was to surprise her with the monies to finally buy their home without having to wait a few more years. To say the least, this incident caused a huge rift between the two of them. Lisa was so angry that she thought about leaving Mike because she felt that he deceived and betrayed her. She began to wonder what else has he hid from her.

Lisa decided to talk to a counselor to sort out her own feelings. Mike joined her in the process with hopes of rebuilding the trust that was damaged. However, their ability to reconnect was largely due to Mike acknowledging that he was wrong even though he was trying to do what he thought was a good thing. After Lisa dealt with the anger and the disappointment through prayer and talking it out with Mike and a counselor, both were able to tap into the grace and forgiveness that they had established as friends before they were married.

The process was long and painful for them both emotionally and financially, but they refused to give up until all was restored. How did they get the intimacy back? By making a choice to do so based on who they knew each other to be in their hearts and because of their own intimate relationship with Christ to be reconciled.

A Jump Start Action Plan
(Feel free to create more of your own action steps
to continue to enhance your marital intimacy)

This week get rid of all the myths that are in your marriage that has been holding the relationship back. For example, letting go of unrealistic expectations and beliefs and develop an intimacy chart that reflects what you two want to see take place in the marriage (ie. a hour of talking about your day everyday before bed).

1. Discover what makes your spouse feel close to you and start giving or doing that special thing today.
2. Recreate a special moment when you were dating that made you both smile.
3. Make sure you kiss and hug for at least five minutes everyday.
4. Learn your spouse's personality for you to know what makes him/her tick and what gets him/her ticked.
5. Celebrate the good in the marriage with a gratitude journal.
6.
7.
8.
9.
10.

Key Points to Remember:

- Know what is true and not true regarding real intimacy.
- Know what your spouse believes about intimacy in comparison to what your believe.
- Decide how to work through intimacy issues once they occur.
- Real intimacy takes works to attain and is even harder to maintain.
- Be willing to share who you really are is the first step to creating real intimacy.

PRAYER

Lord, You are the God of all truth and You desire for us to be truthful with You, ourselves, and with each other. Help us to get rid of all that is false in our lives so that through our truthfulness, we will deepen our bond of trust and intimacy in our marriage. May we experience the rewards of an up close and personal intimacy with the one who is nearest to our heart. In Jesus Name, Amen.

CHAPTER FOUR

Does your marriage have ESP?

"Let the husband render to his wife the affection due her and likewise also the wife to her husband" I Corinthians 7:3 (Holy Bible, New King James Version)

When you hear the initials ESP, what is the first thing that pops into your head? Do psychic powers or a form of paranormal phenomenon immediately come to mind? If this is your understanding of ESP, then let me assure you that I am NOT talking about that kind of ESP at all. The kind of ESP that I am talking about has nothing to do with mystical or telepathic abilities.

Webster's dictionary defines ESP or "extrasensory perception" as the ability for some people to become aware of things by means other than the normal senses. Are we really able to become of aware of things by means other than our normal senses? As a Christian, I believe that God gives us His Holy Spirit to aid and assist us in knowing certain things by no other means than by discernment and insight revealed by the Spirit.

So what do I mean by ESP? ESP is an acronym that I coined when I created a workshop for marriage called "Let's talk about intimacy and sex: Does your marriage have ESP? This whole book is based on the ESP concept that I created for the purpose of discussing the three major components of intimacy that are necessary for building stronger and more solid marriages.

This has all been made possible because of how God created us. According to the scriptures, He created us with a body, soul, and spirit (I Thessalonians 5:23). Our *body* is the "physical house" that we live in and it allows us to live, move, and have our being in the earth realm. The word "soul" comes from the root word "psuche" which is where we get words like psychology or psychosis. The *soul* is the seat of affections, will, desire, emotions, mind, reason, personality, and understanding. Lastly, the *spirit* is the part of us that allows us to connect, respond, and to have a relationship with God.

Therefore, I believe that marriage requires the union of the body, soul, and spirit. It requires that each person in the marital relationship present their "whole self" in their marriage to be fully present and fully engaged. It is possible to know our spouses so well in ways that others do not know them, if we are in tune with one another and in tune with God. He will give us revelation into the heart and soul of our marriages so that we become as one.

In the previous chapters, we have discussed what intimacy is, how intimacy looks in your marriage, how to create intimacy that feels right for you and your spouse, and we have also discussed some intimacy myths. Some of these myths were bought into marriages creating a lack of intimacy in them.

So, what are the three major building blocks for creating a strong and healthy intimate life in a marriage?

The "E" stands for *Emotional Intimacy*. This is the first component of intimacy that relates to the soul union. Emotional Intimacy involves developing closeness through heart-to-heart exchanges of feelings, thoughts, and actions that demonstrates equal expression and acceptance from both partners. Here is where the communication of the soul takes place between the couple.

The "S" stands for *Spiritual Intimacy*. It is the second component of intimacy that relates to the spirit union. Spiritual Intimacy offers the opportunity to nurture the deepest part of each other, that inner self. This type of intimacy provides the essence of life to the relationship because it is connected to the Creator of Life. In other words, the spiritual is what gives meaning and purpose to the "why" of marriage. This is where the "love affair" of the spirit relationship in marriage abides.

Lastly, the "P" stands for *Physical Intimacy*. This is the third component of intimacy that relates to the body union. Physical Intimacy involves the giving and the receiving of marital love, and affection that embodies the sexual experience.

These three components lay the foundation for establishing a great marriage. In the next chapters, we will more fully discuss each ESP component.

What level of intimacy interest you the most and why?

___

Right now, you may be asking yourself, how do we develop this kind of deep connection that is like no other kind of connection on earth? Take time to reflect about how going to the next level in one of the three areas listed above will enhance your marriage. Write what you have discovered about yourself and about your responsibility to change and grow in one of these areas.

___

Key Points to Remember:

- Intimacy is made up of three parts (Emotional, Spiritual, and Physical). These three parts are interrelated. Together they create wholeness by connecting the body, soul (mind, will, emotions), and spirit.
- Marriage is a body, soul, and spirit union.
- All intimacy begins with a true commitment to the marriage.
- Marriage will always demand true intimacy to survive.
- You must learn to connect to the one person with whom you have vowed to spend the rest of your life with. This connection must be in a way that you do not connect with anyone else on earth.

PRAYER

Lord, help us to understand how important it is to make the connection with our minds, bodies and spirits and show us how it affects our marriage relationship. Make our marriage complete in every way. In Jesus Name, Amen.

CHAPTER FIVE

The "E" Factor – EMOTIONAL INTIMACY

"... that you all speak the same thing, and that there be no division among you, but that you be perfectly joined together in the same mind, and in the same judgment" 1 Corinthians 1:10 (Holy Bible, New King James Version)

I love being able to connect with my husband and to share whatever is on my heart. I am extremely grateful that when I do share what is on my heart with him, he validates what I say and how I feel by his willingness to really listen. This lets me know that what I say and how I feel matters to him and that he gets it.

Does this always happen between my husband and I? Does he always get it? Absolutely not! But to be honest, I don't always get him either. It is impossible to always "get it" or for that matter "get it right".

What I have learned over the years is that the most important thing is not whether or not my husband and I "get it" or completely understand what each of us is saying at all times, but that we both feel heard when we try to communicate. That alone, ushers in a calmness to the situation and to each of our hearts. Even if the other person doesn't "get it", the one who is sharing their heart still recognizes that the other person really does care. And that's what emotional intimacy is all about. For me, I could not imagine sharing my most intimate thoughts and feelings with anyone else in the same way that I share them with Keith. With him, I know that I am safe, respected and not judged.

So what is emotional intimacy? **_Emotional Intimacy is a special closeness that is experienced when each person is aware of and acknowledges the other person's feelings_**. Emotional intimacy requires both people to be actively engaged in making the kind of heart connections that grants permission and entrance to that secret place of another. In other words, both parties must be willing to go where no man, or woman for that matter, has dared to go or has even been allowed to access.

In order for emotional intimacy to exist, each person must feel safe enough to become vulnerable and transparent. This feeling of safety invites the one that is closest to us to see our flaws, insecurities, fears, doubts, weaknesses, hurts, and struggles. We must choose to reveal our true selves to our mate, and that includes the good, the bad, and the ugly as well as everything in between. This total openness is how we begin to create an atmosphere for emotional intimacy. I believe that this is what every couple yearns for in their relationship. We need permission to be ourselves and not be afraid or ashamed to show who we are at our worst and knowing that we'll still be loved and accepted. This is true intimacy.

Erica and Roderick found out what true intimacy is all about in their relationship. For Roderick, true intimacy came at a price that required him to expose a part of his past that he is not proud of. A past that he is reminded of everyday.

Some years back, before Roderick and Erica were married, Roderick was arrested for tax evasion and served two years in prison. He followed some bad counsel that he received and that resulted in him not paying his taxes. Roderick believed that he couldn't afford to pay the amount of taxes that he owed, but he soon found out that he really couldn't afford to avoid the expense. As a result of his bad decision, Roderick has a criminal record and it has had an impact on he and Erica's credit score.

Erica never knew that Roderick had served time in prison because he never shared that information. He feared that if she knew about that part of his life, she would not accept him. But Erica did find out

The ESP Marriage

that her husband had spent time in prison when she underwent a credit check to determine her eligibility for a school loan. As a stay-at-home mom, Erica needed the loan to be based on Roderick's income. During the process of securing the school loan, everything was exposed.

Erica was deeply hurt and extremely angry because of Roderick's deliberate deception. Prior to this, Erica felt that she and her husband had the kind of marriage where they could tell each other everything, no matter what. Now, the trust level had eroded between them.

Roderick knew that it was wrong for him to conceal what happened in his past. He acknowledged his failure to come clean about the situation but Erica refuses to forgive. Erica blames Roderick for ruining her chance to go back to school. In addition, she wonders if she can ever trust him again. As the years pass, Erica decides to let go of the hurt and to move forward with life. Love covered the sin that separated them, while creating a bridge to reconnect their lives together again.

Are you experiencing the kind of emotional intimacy that you long for in your marriage? If not, list any obstacles that have caused you to remain closed off from your spouse in this area. Next, beside each obstacle, write down what you believe you need to do to overcome and conquer that obstacle so that it no longer hinders you from making an emotional connection with your mate.

_____
_____
_____
_____
_____
_____
_____

Let's take David and Lena for example. They've struggled for years to develop emotional intimacy. Most of their struggles are due to David not taking the time to listen. "That's why women have girlfriends", he concludes. Besides, David says that when he does try to connect with Lena emotionally, she would become upset because she felt that David always tuned her out.

David doesn't understand that Lena really does want to bond with him, but instead David shuts things down when he feels that the conversation has gone into overtime. David tends to be preoccupied with other plans so he views a drawn out conversation as an inconvenience. It's important that David understands that emotional intimacy takes a lot of time and work. It requires you to check-in with your spouse throughout the day so you can stay constantly connected emotionally. And though it may run into overtime or impact your other plans, know that your spouse is worth the extra effort.

ESP Tip: To achieve emotional intimacy you have to be willing to invest your time. By making yourself available to your spouse, you reinforce their importance and worth.

When you think about your marriage and the emotional intimacy in your relationship, what kinds of emotional investments have you made?

_____
_____
_____
_____
_____
_____
_____
_____

How do you and your spouse plan to make time to invest in the emotional health of your marriage?

_____
_____
_____
_____
_____
_____
_____
_____

The ESP Marriage

What is the most important thing you need to do to build emotional intimacy? Why?

___

On a scale of 1-10, how would rank the emotional intimacy in your marriage?

1 - 2 means no emotional intimacy at all, 3 - 4 means we connect when it is absolutely necessary but not often enough, 5 - 6 means that we are struggling or very little connection, 7 – 8 means things are ok, but could use some improvement here and there, and 9 - 10 means that your relationship is satisfying and fulfilling. Next, explain why you ranked your emotional intimacy at the level that you did.

___

Describe what you can do to make the relationship even better in this area.

___

Finally, write down the things you need from your spouse to help increase the level of emotional intimacy in your marriage.

A Jump Start Action Plan

This week... connect daily with your spouse in a way that is meaningful to both of you. Start by finding out what delights your spouse then do something special – start today! (Feel free to create more of your own action steps to continue to enhance your marital emotional intimacy)

1. Tell each other how much you love one another everyday.
2. Compliment your spouse on something he or she has done for you this week.
3. Write a note about the thing you most admire about your spouse.
4. Ask what you can do to assist your spouse with household chores.
5. Make phone calls to each other throughout the day.
6.
7.
8.
9.
10.

Key Points to Remember:

- Make a commitment to invest time to achieve true emotional intimacy.
- True emotional intimacy should not be rushed.
- "Be real" and "keep it real" with one another.
- Ensure that trust and safety are key components for establishing emotional intimacy.
- Acknowledge where you and your spouse need help in the area of emotional intimacy.
- Devise a plan to improve this area of your relationship.
- Do at least one thing daily to improve the quality of the emotional health of your marriage.

PRAYER

Lord, connect my spouse and I in a way that creates and strengthens our emotional intimacy one with another. Show us how to give unselfishly of ourselves with our time so that we offer whole-heartedly our undivided attention in order to grow together and understand each other fully.
In Jesus Name, Amen.

CHAPTER SIX

The "S" Factor – SPIRITUAL INTIMACY

And the Lord God caused a deep sleep to fall on Adam and he slept; and He took one of his ribs, and closed up the flesh in its place. Then the rib, which the Lord God had taken from man, He made into a woman, and He brought her to the man. And Adam said..."This is now bone of my bones and flesh of my flesh." Then God blessed them... Genesis 2:21-23a; 1:28. (Holy Bible, New King James Version)

Nowadays, it seems everyone is looking for a soul mate. I've often wondered if the people who are on the lookout for their soul mate really know what they're in search of. What does having a "soul mate" really mean?

Webster defines "soul mate" as one or two persons of the opposite sex temperamentally suited to each other. This definition lacks what I feel is the true connotation behind what people really mean when they talk about a soul mate. It certainly does not define nor illustrate what I believe a soul mate is and it certainly does not address where the concept of a "soul mate" originated.

Well, I believe that the word "soul" and "mate" originated in the beginning when God created man and woman for each other in the Garden of Eden. The scripture says that Eve came "out of"

Adam. In other words, she came out of the deepest part of him. How she arrived on the scene depicts how vital her existence is to man. The depth of her origin defines the spiritual purpose that she was designed to have in connection with her man so much so that she is the only one who can truly relate to him and respond to his deepest needs like none other.

Perhaps that is why growing together spiritually is one of the greatest gifts that you give to yourself and to your spouse. The oneness is where the true meaning of soul mate comes to fruition. This is where the strongest of all bonds takes place and forms the building blocks for a strong foundation. Such closeness sets the stage for spiritual intimacy and gives purpose to the marriage.

So, what is spiritual intimacy? ***Spiritual Intimacy is connecting and penetrating the very soul and spirit of one another. It is when you view your marriage as a gift from God that is to be treasured not only as something very special, honorable, and good but also sacred.***

There is great nourishment that comes from a spiritually unified relationship. Spiritual Intimacy allows couples to see their marriage as a private world all its own to be used as a source of healing and growth. Therefore, I believe that spiritual intimacy becomes the essence from which we live our lives together being synchronized in the spirit.

How would you describe spiritual intimacy?
_____
_____
_____
_____
_____
_____
_____
_____

The ESP Marriage

If you could draw a picture of what your spiritual life looks like in your marriage, what would that be? Why?

_____
_____
_____
_____
_____
_____
_____
_____

ESP TIP: Prioritize spiritual intimacy in your marriage. Don't let it become the last thing on your "to-do list".

As couples learn each other and become more in tune with one another spiritually, a special closeness is formed that joins them in new ways that creates ultimate intimacy. Their close union helps the couple deepen their relationship with God both as individuals and as a couple.

To further illustrate this, let's visit Karen and Ronald. This couple had a great relationship with God individually but struggled in developing spiritual intimacy together. Yes, they went to church together, sang the same songs together and read from the same bible together. Yet, the only time that they actually prayed together was during dinnertime and the only other time that they really ever talked about God was when someone they knew died.

Karen believes that being close spiritually is important to the relationship. However, Ronald was taught that religion is a personal matter and felt no real need to go beyond what they were already doing together. The real problem was much deeper than this. Ronald felt intimidated about trying to lead the home spiritually because he really didn't know what was expected of him. Besides, he always believed that Karen was so much more qualified to lead the home spiritually than he was because she seemed to know the bible better than he did.

Karen began to feel the spiritual burden of things especially when her father became ill and she was the primary caregiver. Not knowing what the outcome would be regarding her father's health, she needed that extra reassurance that God cares. Yet, it was hard for her to pray or read the bible or for that matter to concentrate on God's faithfulness in her life.

Ronald began to notice how her father's illness was affecting her mood, her energy level, and her peace of mind. He asked Karen how he could help her? She answered by asking him to read scriptures to her. Soon, Ronald found himself becoming more and more comfortable reading the scriptures aloud, which later led him to begin to pray over his wife with ease.

By Ronald stepping up to the plate and giving his wife what she needed, he established himself in the spiritual position that he once shied away from. Ronald realized that spiritual oneness begins with taking small steps daily.

Have you felt like something was missing in the area of spiritual intimacy with your spouse? If so, describe it and write down ways you can make improvements in the area.

_____
_____
_____
_____
_____
_____
_____

Spiritual intimacy is largely determined by the importance that both people place on it from the very beginning of their relationship (you remember those premarital classes, don't you?). If both of you are Christians, maybe you assumed that God would be a priority in the marriage. But like anything else, spiritual intimacy isn't automatic, developing it takes effort.

Perhaps spiritual intimacy is a challenge because the level of faith or closeness to God that you experience isn't in sync with your spouse. If that's the case, the two of you must work together to get on the same page.

How important is it for you to feel connected to your spouse spiritually?

_____
_____
_____
_____
_____
_____
_____
_____

What role does spirituality play in your marriage?

_____
_____
_____
_____
_____
_____
_____

When Keith and I were dating, I can remember when we decided to pray with one another one night after going out together. Well, when we started our prayer time, I initially played it safe. I only exposed that which made me look "saintly" or "super spiritual". Then, Keith prayed and started confessing things that I thought was too personal to share, especially with someone that he was just dating. But it revealed to me that he was serious about his relationship with God and me. His actions said, "if we are going to pray, then let's pray."

To be honest, I was literally shocked at some of the things that Keith said in prayer. He showed me that he was comfortable with himself. He also showed me that he trusted me enough to give me a peek into his soul so that we could journey together in truth. He realized early in our relationship that if we were going to be spiritually connected then we had to be willing to take risks.

If you long for spiritual intimacy with your mate, then you must risk being true to yourself and your spouse regardless of what each of you may think.

***ESP TIP:** You must also consider that spiritual intimacy is based on how comfortable each person feels in opening up and sharing in this way.*

A Jump Start Action Plan
(Feel free to create more of your own action steps
to continue to enhance your marital spiritual intimacy)

This week...establish or strengthen a spiritual foundation in your marriage by identifying where you both are and where you both need to grow. Start by talking about it with one another.

1 Make a decision to pray for each other for five minutes a day.
2. Buy a new bible/book to read together such as a couples devotional guide.
3. Attend a conference/couples' retreat that will encourage spiritual growth.
3. Ask other friends for new ideas.
4. Write a mission statement for your marriage.
5. Affirm your marriage with positive words regarding who you two are and who you two will become in the future.
6.
7.
8.
9.
10.

Consider today what true spiritual intimacy requires. My belief is that in order to know what true intimacy is, it involves a personal relationship with the Lord. He alone is the one that created the very longings of our soul to love and to be loved completely. The bible says we love because He first loved us (I John 4:19). God demonstrated the beginning and ending of all love by dying on the cross for us. That is real love! So God must be apart of the love equation since He created love.

Since God is love and just as God loves us, He expects us to do likewise. Therefore, husbands are to love their wives just as Christ loved the church and gave Himself for her and therefore, wives are to see that she respects her husband (Ephesians 5:25, 33).

Do you believe that a relationship with God is necessary in developing a close and intimate relationship in your marriage? Why or why not?

_____
_____
_____
_____
_____
_____
_____
_____

Key Points to Remember:

- Emphasize how important spiritual intimacy is for your marriage by making it a priority.
- True soul mates originated with God so make sure He is included in your pursuit of real spiritual intimacy.
- Spiritual intimacy is not automatic. You must work to develop it.
- Spiritual intimacy is a building block for establishing a strong foundation in a marriage.
- Spiritual intimacy requires that you get out of your comfort zone and dare to take the spiritual journey of truth together. In other words, be willing to develop new practices such as journaling that can deepen your spiritual life.

PRAYER

Lord, help me and _____ to become true "soul mates" by first surrendering our lives to You completely and then to one another spiritually. Our desire is to be acquainted with each other so intimately that we capture the essence of who we are individually and who we are meant to be as a couple. In Jesus name, Amen.

CHAPTER SEVEN

The "P" Factor – PHYSICAL INTIMACY

"I am my beloved's and his desire is towards me. Let him kiss me with kisses of his mouth...for your love is better than wine" (Song of Solomon 7:10, 1:2) Holy Bible, New King James Bible.

Desire. Who doesn't have desire? Everyone has a desire for something. But the desire that I'm talking about is a desire to be loved, to be wanted, to be embraced, to be consumed with the passion experienced in the oneness of bodies melted into one another. This type of desire describes the intense intimacy created within a marriage for the fulfillment and enjoyment that comes from physical intimacy. Excuse me, is it getting hot in here or is it just me? Whew!!!

What do you desire? If you want to know what real desire looks like, read the Bible's Song of Solomon. I love this book because it depicts the intimate love relationship between a husband and wife who are madly in love with each other. They have a longing for one another that seems to be unquenchable. Only one person can quench this kind of longing, "The Beloved". What is a beloved? Webster's defines "beloved" as dearly loved. Are you the beloved in your marriage? Do you feel dearly loved? Take some time to think about what it means to be the "beloved".

The ESP Marriage

In my marriage, I know what it is to be the beloved and I know what it is to desire my husband. For me, I desire my husband the way I desire chocolate. To say that I love chocolate is an understatement. I mean, I really, really love chocolate—the strong bold aroma beckons me, the smooth dark appearance seduces me, the rich creamy flavor excites my taste buds, and the warm and cozy way that I feel after I have surrendered myself to it is the ultimate indulgence. Sometimes my craving for chocolate is so intense that once I give into the craving, the feeling of satisfaction and fulfillment is indescribable. Ooh... how I want a piece of chocolate right now just thinking about it. If you had to describe the "desire" for physical intimacy in your marriage, what food would you choose to illustrate it? Explain why you chose this food.

_____
_____
_____
_____
_____
_____
_____

To put it simply, physical intimacy is about being desired by your beloved and feeling dearly loved in return. Physical intimacy means different things to different people. However, there is one thing that I want to be clear on and that is that physical intimacy is not just about sex, though it certainly does include sex. Don't get me wrong, physical contact or touch is vital to the health and security of any and all marriages. However, *physical intimacy includes loving and affectionate touching, warm embraces, deep kissing, and the passionate intertwining of bodies for the purpose of sexual fulfillment and satisfaction and not just for procreation.* So don't confine your perception of physical intimacy to just focus on penetration when it includes much, much, more than that.

How would describe the physical intimacy in your marriage?

_____
_____
_____
_____
_____
_____
_____
_____

Is there a component of physical intimacy that is missing or lacking in your marriage? If yes, describe what it is and why you think it is missing or lacking.

_____
_____
_____
_____
_____
_____
_____
_____

God is the creator of sex. And just like everything else that He created, God said it was good. Yet, that does not mean that everything is going to be perfect in this area. Perhaps, you and your spouse have encountered some problems in this area. Physical intimacy issues may result from bad experiences, and/or a faulty belief system.

The truth is, some people may have had some traumatic things to happen to them in this area that may impede their ability to function sexually. It could be due to a rape or a molestation that occurred while growing up, or as a result of some other form of abuse that occurred in their lives. Whatever the circumstances were or are, it certainly can play a major role in how couples experience physical intimacy or the lack thereof.

Such tragic events can certainly inhibit couples from having a positive perspective regarding sex as a good thing because of the pain that is associated with it. Those who have experienced such a violation sometimes find it very difficult to move forward from that place of hurt. They may also find it difficult to feel good about themselves or to feel safe about giving themselves wholly to their spouse because they have not fully been healed over their past.

Or, perhaps there are some faulty belief systems that are in place from one or both of the couples past that continues to be played over and over again. These very thoughts can cause marriages to stay stuck in the area of physical intimacy. Some faulty beliefs may include things such as: sex is only for procreation, sex is nasty, only certain positions are allowed, good girls don't do that, or it is easier to give sex than to become intimate, on and on the list goes.

Maybe some of the beliefs may have been derived from TV, magazines, books, and movies that offer a superficial version of a physical expression of love. These versions lacks in expressing the depth of physical intimacy of the covenant marriage commitment which is to share the ultimate gift of one special person's body. This includes forsaking all others with the intent purpose of totally being with and satisfying only one person...the beloved.

These faulty beliefs form behaviors that may keep couples from capturing the type of love God had in mind for them. By discovering what the foundational beliefs are about intimacy, couples can learn the right tools to conquer any faulty beliefs or fears that they have and eliminate the old bad recordings that may be playing over and over again in their minds.

Regardless how these faulty belief systems came about whether they were past down from friends, family, or the church you need to identify those beliefs that are contrary to what God intends for you and your spouse to enjoy freely in your marriage. Begin to create new beliefs based on what you may want and know to be true that is derived from what the bibles says as well as what you two agree on and believe is right for the two of you.

Whatever the circumstances or issues that surround you and your spouse from having a healthy and passionate sex life, seek professional services. Such services will assist the two of you in overcoming barriers and that can lead to healing and wholeness. Please refer to the back of this book for the resource section. This section recommends helpful books and websites for growing and developing happy marriages.

ESP TIP: Work the problem; don't let the problem work you! In other words, identify and deal with the problem at hand without letting it rule and/or ruin your marriage.

What about other types of issues that disrupts the flow of physical intimacy in the marriages? Some of those issues may include things like the amount or frequency of sex in the marriage or it could be communication problems or male impotence. What other issues can sometimes interrupt sexual intimacy? Let's look at just four marital dilemmas.

Physical Exhaustion

Kristie and Steven have always had an enjoyable sex life until she had a baby. Lately, Steven seems to want more sex more often in spite of how tired Kristie is since becoming a mother. Kristie has had no desire for sex at all. This bothers her as much as it does Steven. Yet, Kristie feels like she has so much to do in trying to meet the needs of the baby, work, and managing the household. So for her the thought of sex is exhausting even more so than the energy to actually have sex. This issue has created an environment of constant arguing between the two of them.

Now Kristie is starting to feel like Steven is disrespecting her by his persistent pressure for sex. Steven's disregard to how Kristie feels physically has Kristie frustrated, angry, and filled with resentment. Steven feels that Kristie is just using excuses for not wanting to have sex. He believes that she is consumed with everything and everybody but their relationship. As far as Steven is concerned, sex is not that important to Kristie. He feels that she has placed him at the bottom of her list of things to do. Steven states that "it seems that she rather invest her time in meeting the needs of others than meeting his needs".

A close friend of Kristie suggested that they go and talk to someone who could probably help them to overcome this problem.

The pastor suggested that Kristie tell Steven what it is that she needs from him. He also suggested that she explain to her husband how he could assist her so that she would have more energy and time to spend with him.

For Kristie, having Steven address some of her needs would help to restore their sex life. At first, it was hard for Steven to view himself as being inconsiderate just because he wants to have sex with his wife. It took a couple of sessions of counseling for Steven to see what life has been like from Krisitie's perspective. Steven acknowledged his selfishness and his insensitivity towards Kristie and asked for forgiveness. He promised to help her with the many tasks that she had often done alone so that they could reconnect in their relationship. It seems the couple has made a wonderful first effort but for a true physical connection to occur, they need to make this a priority in their marriage.

ESP TIP: Schedule time to "make love" happen!

Let's look at another issue some couples face...

Boredom

Brian and Jessica had a problem with boredom in the bedroom. Things used to be so hot and exciting but not anymore. There used to be a time when they couldn't wait to release the uninhibited passion that they both enjoyed sharing with one another. Yet, it seems like things have cooled off lately. In fact, things are so cool for the both of them that they are almost sexually cold towards each other.

Brian and Jessica have gotten used to having sex in the same place, at the same time, in the same way. The fire of passion still flickers some but the routine of sex has begun to feel more like a chore or something done out of obligation. Brian and Jessica never talked to each other about their sex life. Although both felt that something was missing, they realized that something new needed to take place.

The reason why Brian and Jessica did not make any changes in this area of their lives was because they really didn't know quite what to do. Although they both wanted change, they both feared rejection or perhaps offending each other with certain suggestions or requests. One weekend, Jessica attended a women's conference that spoke about this very issue. She learned that men are visually stimulated and that women are emotionally stimulated when it comes to sex. That weekend, Jessica received great ideas that she was anxious to share with Brian and even more anxious to actually try in the bedroom. One of the ideas involved buying a belly-dancing outfit, and some belly dancing music, to dance an exotic, yet sensual dance in front of her husband as a delicious surprise.

Jessica bravely tried this idea out one night with Brian. Brian could not believe how good Jessica looked. He forgot how sensual she could really be and how the whole experience was very seductively alluring for them both. That night they made love as they never made love before.

This opened up dialog between the two of them to discuss each other's sexual likes, wants, and needs without any inhibitions. Jessica and Brian both began to think up new ideas based on what they'd communicated to each other earlier. They began creating their own intimate fantasies. In fact, they were both willing to fulfill those fantasies with each other thus capturing the deep intimate pleasures of marital love. The couple's openness to try something new, took Jessica's and Brian's physical intimacy to a higher level.

ESP TIP: *Using your imagination can spark unimaginable ideas for having great sex. Don't neglect the greatest sex organ in the human body...the brain!*

Are you bored in your physical intimacy? Brainstorm together and come up with some creative ways to spice things up.

1.
2.
3.
4.
5.

CAUTION: THE RULES FOR MAKING LOVE IS TO NEVER PARTAKE IN ANY SEXUAL ACTIVITY WITH EACH OTHER, IF EITHER HUSBAND OR WIFE FEELS UNCOMFORTABLE, VIOLATED OR BELIEVES THAT A PARTICULAR ACT IS IMMORAL.

Another couple faces...Impotence

Joel and Donna have been happily married for twenty-eight years with a healthy sex life. However, lately Joel has been having difficulty getting an erection and maintaining it throughout the sexual encounter with Donna. Initially, Donna felt like Joel was in denial because when Donna tried to talk to Joel about their sexual struggles, he became frustrated and shut down.

Donna wondered whether or not Joel was not getting enough stimulation during foreplay. Or, maybe it was something else... like losing his desire for her. But after a long conversation with each other, Joel confessed that he didn't like to talk about this because it made him feel like he was old. He felt as if this meant that he could no longer satisfy Donna, which caused him to feel slightly embarrassed. Joel did not like the fact that he was no longer in control of his body and the thought of using something artificial to help him have and keep an erection made him feel less of a "real man".

Donna suggested to Joel that maybe he should go to the doctor to get a check up and find out what's really going on. Joel took Donna's advice and found out that he has what is known as "ED" or Erectile Dysfunction. The doctor shared several options with Joel and Donna to help them overcome this problem and to resume a healthy sex life. The couple took one of the doctor's suggestions so they could move forward in their lives.

ESP TIP: Don't give up hope. Find out if your sexual problems are in need of medical or psychological intervention. This could include your primary care doctor, a counselor or sex therapist.

A final dilemma...Insecurity

Sex between Tony and Adrian was never really that great. This was due mainly to Adrian's recent weight gain. Over the years, Adrian has become more self-conscious about her body especially during intercourse. Tony often tells Adrian that the weight does not matter, but she didn't believe him.

For Adrian, her weight has been the cause for her not feeling or acting sexy towards Tony. It has also been the reason for her lack of creativity in the bedroom. Adrian felt like her weight issue was "the issue" especially after a remark that Tony made one night during foreplay. One night, Tony, in a loving fun way told Adrian how much he loved her big juicy thighs. Instead of taking his comment as a compliment, Adrian felt as though Tony was really saying that she was fat.

Unfortunately, this comment turned Adrian off and never quite turned her back on. Although she knew that he was just being playful, she could not seem to get over it. At first, Tony felt as if Adrian was overreacting until she told him how much the comment hurt her. Even though Tony expressed the comment as a "cute sensuous sentiment," he realized that what he had intended as a compliment really hurt his wife. When he noticed just how much this offended her, he apologized. He admitted that he honestly meant nothing by it. He promised he would never do it again. But, by that time, the damage had been done.

Since that time, Tony feared making any kind of comment that has anything to do with her body. And as for Adrian, she became even more insecure about her size, resulting in her not acting her usual self, sexually. How might Adrian and Tony resolve this issue?

What might be helpful is for Tony to compliment Adrian in a nonsexual way by telling her the things that he loves about her. This will make her feel like the focus is not on her body or body parts but on her as a person. Tony could demonstrate this by showing Adrian that he appreciates and adores all of her. Perhaps this will cause her to feel more confident about herself and her size.

ESP TIP: Deal with self-esteem issues head on. Build confidence by focusing on your strengths instead of your weaknesses.

If any of these problems existed between you and your spouse, what would you do to solve the dilemma?

_____
_____
_____
_____
_____
_____
_____

A Jump Start Action Step

This week…use all of your senses to explore and celebrate a delicious expression of physical intimacy. Create a visual storyboard about the kind of sexual experience you'd like to have happen for the two of you tonight. (For example, cut out a picture of the Eiffel Tower to illustrate the height of ecstasy).

(Feel free to create more of your own action steps to continue to enhance your marital physical intimacy)

1. Read an erotic book of poetry together on marital love.
2. Role play a special date or a favorite romantic scene from a movie.
3. Call on the phone and whisper sexual fantasies waiting at home.
4. Create a new you…new lingerie, hairstyle, and scent, creates a new attitude.
5. Plan for a quickie in the middle of the day.
6. Awaken your spouse with a pleasurable stimulus in the middle of the night.
7. Cook in the nude (ensure that no one else is in the house first) or sleep in the nude.
8. Make love in a different location.
9. Share what you love about each other's bodies.
10. Give a great body massage from top to bottom.
11.
12.
13.
14.
15.
16.
17.
18.
19.
20.

Key Points to Remember:

- Physical intimacy is more than about sex.
- Communicate about how to solve intimate problems.
- Use creativity to keep things hot and spicy.
- Treat each other as the "Beloved". Express love, value, worth, and respect for one another that will spill over into physical intimacy.
- Desire for each other only releases the reward of pure ecstasy in the bedroom.
- Seek professional help for sexual dysfunctions.
- Include God in your sexual relationship...remember He is the one who created it.

PRAYER

Lord, your word says that every good and perfect gift comes from you and we know that sex is one of those gifts. Help us to enjoy sex in our marriage the way you intended for it to be. Help us to make the time to spend with each other, talking and understanding what we both desire and need in order to fulfill one another's needs unselfishly. Help us to keep our vow of physical intimacy pure and fresh. And let us always be the "Beloved" in each other's lives now and forever. In Jesus name, Amen.

CHAPTER EIGHT

Growing in ESP for a Lifetime of Intimacy

"How great is God's goodness to have given you to me to love for a lifetime" ~Anonymous

Marriage is a beautiful thing and I love being married!!! I am grateful for the wonderful ESP that my husband and I have enjoyed in our marriage and yet we are still growing in our intimate relationship. Since the majority of our married life has been as a military couple enduring challenges such as frequent deployments and war, we've had to work hard at maintaining our ESP connection. Nevertheless, we look forward to building a lifetime of continuous intimacy in our marriage.

Like every marriage, we have encountered our share of ups and downs. And although we have experienced challenges, we consider our marriage *perfect*. Yes, we know that there is no such thing as a perfect marriage, but I am talking about perfect in the sense that we are "perfect" for each other.

Over the years, we have learned to accept each other's imperfections without trying to change one another. Believe me, we tried that and it just doesn't work. When you try to change your spouse, you're just wasting your time. All it does is create frustration between the two of you, which then turns into a battle of the wills. People want to be loved just the way they are.

You may ask how we got to the place where we accepted each other just the way we are. You also may be wondering how long it took us to get there. For us, we needed to shift our focus from what is wrong about one another to focus on what is right about each other. We also began to improve ourselves so that each of us would become the type of marriage partner that we desire and need. I encourage you to become the type of spouse that you want and you are sure to get what you want and need from your partner.

But don't look for an instant fix. The process of building a "perfect" marriage is ongoing. It requires learning about each other, learning the lessons from the mistakes made, and being willing to grow together with patience, understanding and forgiveness. Developing a lifetime of ESP takes a lot of work—hard work. Be ready to roll up your sleeves and dig in your heels.

Part of the challenge comes when you and your spouse identify the obstacles that have been hindering your intimacy from the start. These are what I call the "ESP BUSTERS". These "ESP BUSTERS" can prevent married couples from achieving a lifetime of intimacy because they block the flow of intimacy. But once you've learned how to navigate through them successfully, they will no longer have a presence in your relationship. You may even forget they ever existed.

Let's look at a few of the ESP BUSTERS and then learn ways to deal with them effectively.

Emotional Intimacy Buster:

- Lack of communication (talking and listening)
- Not being affectionate
- Lack of trust
- Being too needy or clingy
- Negativity (criticizing)
- No respect
- Too controlling
- Lack of time (being too busy for the good of the relationship)
- Blame game
- Lack of sensitivity

Listed above are a few Emotional Intimacy Busters. What do you see as an emotional buster in your marriage? List as many as you can.

_____
_____
_____
_____
_____
_____
_____
_____

Once you and your spouse have identified the ESP Intimacy Busters in your marriage, come up with a plan to master them together. For example, if you and your spouse are dealing with Emotional Busters perhaps the two of you could:

- Learn how to communicate with each other by expressing things in a way in which the other person needs to hear it.

- Share the love…say it and show it everyday by speaking words of love that caress your mate's soul.

- Avoid doing anything or saying anything that promotes dishonesty and a lack of trust.

- Give each other space to connect with themselves.

- Watch out for the words, actions, and feelings that are negative. Proverbs 18:21 says life and death are in the power of the tongue. So be uplifting or encouraging by speaking life.

- Always show respect each other in word and deed.

- Don't try to control each other with fear and manipulation. Allow each person to own who they are.

> Slow down and make time for each other everyday.

> Take responsibility for your own actions and reactions.

> Show you care by validating each other by listening to one another and honoring each other's feelings. This increases deposits in the love bank of the your marriage.

One biblical key to remember for developing emotional intimacy is found in I Peter 3:8-9. That particular verse talks about an effort taken to work towards being of one mind, having compassion for one another, and love…being tenderhearted, courteous, and not returning evil for evil… but on the contrary a blessing. (Paraphrased) This is a verse that I feel summarizes emotional intimacy quite well because it stresses what main elements are necessary for establishing and sustaining emotional intimacy. Employing this truth provides a marriage with a strong emotional bond.

Spiritual Intimacy Busters:

- Dogmatic (Imposing on your spouse)
- Self-Righteous
- Judgmental
- Legalistic (Rules)
- Fanatical (Lack of spiritual balance)
- Outside Influences
- Hypocritical

Listed above are a few Spiritual Intimacy Busters. What do you see as a spiritual buster in your marriage? List as many as you can.

_____
_____
_____
_____
_____
_____
_____

When it comes to dealing with Spiritual Intimacy Busters, there are several ways to handle them. Some tools to utilize for eliminating these busters in your relationship are:

- Learn to agree to disagree regarding how each other may understand or believe certain aspects of their faith or spiritual journey. Be flexible and open to an opposing viewpoint.

- Remember, no one is perfect. No matter where each of us are in our spiritual walk, we all still require help and guidance from God. We are all a work in progress and will need to continue to make changes within ourselves so we can grow.

- Judge not so that you will not be judge (Matthew 7:1). Meaning you cannot judge someone motives, only actions.

- Lay off the rules and focus on the spiritual relationship and bond.

- Create the spiritual balance that is needed to be able to relate to one another when it comes to spiritual matters or just real life.

- Don't let others influence you and your spouse's spiritual walk with each other and with God.

- Be for real in your spirituality. Live what you say you are!

To develop a strong and vibrant spiritual relationship within a marriage, it is important for Christian couples to believe in the same God (Jesus). It is also important to agree to live according to the bible and the principles taught for a successful marriage and life.

Physical Intimacy Busters:

- Refusing to have sex
- Comparing past sexual experiences
- Not discussing each other's sexual likes and dislikes
- Lack of sensitivity (what personally feels right, comfortable and is consensual)
- Lack of an emotional connection
- Excuses (ie. too tired)
- Boredom
- Kids
- Unresolved anger
- Infidelity

Listed above are a few Physical Intimacy Busters. What do you see are some physical intimacy busters in your marriage? List as many as you can.

_____
_____
_____
_____
_____

Physical Intimacy Busters can create huge problems in a marriage and these issues must be resolved. There are a myriad of solutions that can be used to remedy the physical problems that can kill the sex life of a marriage. Let's consider a few…

➢ If one partner is refusing to have sex, find out why by talking about it. If the two of you cannot resolve the problem, get a third person involved such as a counselor.

➢ Let the past stay in the past especially if it includes former sexual relationships. There is no value in comparing your spouse with another person. It only incites hurt, anger, bitterness, and resentment.

- Ask about each other's likes and dislikes so that your lovemaking experience can be an expression of true giving and receiving.

- Sex is not about being selfish. Remember it is not all about YOU. Be sensitive to each other's needs without pressuring the other person to do something that makes them feel uncomfortable or violated.

- Sex begins outside the bedroom. Do what it takes to be connected and feel connected to your spouse emotionally before ever trying to connect sexually. Learn the lost art of verbal lovemaking.

- Excuses are reasons for justifying why people don't do certain things. Deal with the truth when it comes to not wanting to have sex. Let the other person know exactly what you need (ie. help with the kids, a little extra sleep, help with the house) to alleviate excuses ruining your sex life.

- If the two of you are bored, agree on what to do to put more excitement and adventure into your lovemaking. Explore how to become closer sexually to bring greater satisfaction. And remember what Hebrews 13:4 says about marriage... marriage is honorable among all, and the bed undefiled.

- Ensure your children have a daily routine with a schedule so that you can spend intimate time with your spouse.

- Deal with unresolved anger so that it will not stifle your desire to be with one another. Forgiveness is a major key in overcoming any kind of hurt. If that is too difficult to do alone, seek professional help.

- Infidelity is the greatest betrayal in a marriage relationship. However, many couples have been able to overcome it and get back on track. The healing process may not happen overnight, but if both couples are willing, forgiveness and reconciliation can take place.

The scripture stresses how important the sexual relationship is between the husband and wife. It also emphasizes that neither spouse should deprive the other of it. However, there is an exception to every rule. The rule for married couples to abstain from sex requires both people to agree that for a limited time only, no sexual activity will take place if one person feels a need to deal with spiritual matters by fasting and praying. This should never be done for selfish reasons (I Corinthians 7:5). Of course, if there are medical reasons involved that interrupts the sexual relationship, then those issues should be adhered to as well. Other than for those particular reasons, sex should be a very vital part of the marriage union.

The same scripture also highlights that a lack of sexual activity brings greater temptation to the marriage. Therefore, maintaining a regular sex life can prevent possible infidelities from entering the marriage and causing irreparable damage to a relationship. So preserve and protect all areas of intimacy in your marriage—including your sex life so that you can enjoy the best of ESP for a lifetime.

ESP TIP: Lifetime intimacy is a work in progress. It doesn't happen overnight so be patient. Give everything you have to develop ESP because your marriage deserves it.

A Jump Start Action Plan
(Feel free to create more of your own action steps
to continue to enhance your lifetime of ESP intimacy)

1. Imagine what you want your marriage to look like five, ten, or even thirty years from now. What would you have to do in order for you to have a strong ESP marriage?

2. Identify the ESP BUSTERS in your marriage and do something to rid your relationship of them by finding workable solutions that are right for you and your spouse.

3. Try to learn something new about your spouse this week in one of the three areas of ESP.

4. Think of two things that you could change about yourself that would benefit the marriage.

5. Challenge your marriage to grow in an area that the two of you feel stuck.

6. Do something new together in each area of ESP that will enrich the relationship.

7. Discover your spouses love language by reading *The Five Love Languages* by Gary Chapman.

8. Highlight your spouse's greatest virtues above those of others.

9. Plan regular times throughout the year to get away with your spouse to be refreshed emotional, spiritually and physically.

10. Renew your marriage vows in the intimacy of your own home over a romantic dinner or in bed.

11.

12.

13.

14.

15.

16.

17.

18.

19.

20.

Key Points to Remember:

- Accept your spouse without trying to change him or her.
- Choose a battle you can win…change yourself.
- Become what you want in a spouse and you are sure to get what you want and need in your partner.
- Developing ESP is an ongoing process.
- "ESP BUSTERS" if not identified and dealt with can destroy intimacy.
- Continue to grow in understanding and knowledge of one another to enhance the ESP in your marriage.
- Work daily to create long lasting intimacy.

PRAYER

Lord, you said marriage is honorable among all therefore, we desire to honor You in our marriage. Since marriage is Your idea and everything You made you've placed eternal value on it, only You can help us to make it last for a lifetime. Help us to understand the worth of our marriage as well as the purpose for marriage. Open our eyes so that we will continue to value it enough to work hard at creating a great marriage and to leave a great legacy behind. Give us a lifetime of ESP in our marriage with our soul mate until death do us part.

In Jesus name, Amen.

AFTERWORD

If you have longed to experience *real* intimacy in your marriage, my HOPE for you is that The ESP Marriage book has helped you and your spouse realize that desire. If you and your spouse have struggled in trying to make the connection in the areas of emotional, spiritual, or physical intimacy with little or no progress, my PRAYER is that you and your spouse's struggles are over and that The ESP concepts has enabled you two to make the connection that has enriched and revitalized your marriage.

Remember, developing true intimacy is a process, so be encouraged! Most couples have struggled in some area of intimacy in their marriage. However, you can reposition your marriage to overcome these challenges and grow more in tune and more in love with one another from the insights gained from *The ESP Marriage* book.

I sincerely hope that your marriage relationship will continue to celebrate a lifelong and satisfying union by implementing the tips, exercises, and prayers found in this book. May these tools benefit your relationship by keeping you and your spouse focused and on track for designing a strong, committed, and an incredibly intimate marriage for the two of you to richly enjoy!!!

I invite you to share with me any comments or testimonies regarding how this book has changed you and your marriage. I would love to hear from you. You can contact me at www.nturner@uniquelydesignedcoaching.com. Also check out my website at www.uniquelydesignedcoaching.com for upcoming events, speaking engagements, teleclasses, and/or feel free to ask me a question regarding your marriage or whatever is on your heart.

May God bless your pursuit towards achieving a great "ESP Marriage"!

RECOMMENDED READING AND RESOURCES

Balon, R. & Segraves, R. (2005). *Handbook of sexual dysfunction.* Boca Raton, FL: Taylor and Fracis Group, LLC.

Black, S. (2002). *Can two walk together? – Encouragement for spiritually unbalanced marriage.* Printed in the United States of America.

Beck, M. & Beck, S. et al. (1999). *365 Questions for couples.* Hollbrook, MA: Adams Media Corporation.

Chapman, G. (1992). *The five love languages: How to express heartfelt commitment to your mate.* Chicago, IL: Northfield Publishing.

Dillow, J. (1977). *Solomon on sex: The biblical guide to married love.* Nashville, TN: Thomas Nelson Publishers.

Enright, R. D. (2001). *Forgiveness Is a Choice: A step-by-step process for resolving anger and restoring hope.* Washington, DC: American Psychological Association.

Ferguson, D. & Ferguson, T. (2001). *The one year book of devotions.* Carol Stream, IL: Tyndale House Publishers.

Harley, W. F. (2001). *His Needs, Her Needs* (15th ed.) Grand Rapids, MI: Fleming H. Revell.

Jakes, T. D. (2000). *The Great Investment: Faith, Family, and Finance*. New York, NY: G. P. Putnam's Sons.

Medicine Net
www.medicinenet.com
Medicinenet is an online health care media publishing company

Morley, P. (1994). *Devotions for couples: For busy couples who want more intimacy in their relationships*. Grand Rapids, MI: Zondervan Publishing House.

New King James Bible (1991). *Spirit filled life bible*. Nashville, TN: Thomas Nelson Publishers.

Parrot, L. & Parrot, L. (2002). *The love list*. Grand Rapids, MI: Zondervan Publisher.

Schlessinger, L. (2004). *The proper care and feeding of husbands*. New York, NY: Harper Collins Publishers, Inc.

Stoop, D. & Stoop, J. (2002). *The complete marriage book*. Grand Rapids, MI: Revell.

U.S. Department of Health and Human Services – Administration for Children and Families for Healthy Marriage Initiative

www.acf.hhs.gov/healthymarriage

Healthy Marriage Initiative is a website offering marriage education services to help couples acquire the skills and knowledge necessary to form and sustain a healthy marriage.

Weiss, D. (2003). *Intimacy: A 100-day guide to lasting relationships*. Lake Mary, FL: Strang Communications Company.

Yandian, B. (1993). *One flesh: God's Gift of Passion – Love, sex, and romance in marriage.* Orlando, FL: Creation House Publishers.

BIOGRAPHY

Nashawn Turner, M.A., is the President of Uniquely Designed Coaching, LLC., a personal and professional development and life coaching business dedicated to empowering women to redesign their lives to fit their life's purpose. She is a Certified Life Coach, a Counselor and a professional motivational and inspirational speaker. Many refer to her as the "Marriage Coach" due to her popular and sought-out workshops on marriage. Her passion for marriage now highlights her and her husband in a national campaign sponsored by the National Fatherhood Initiative called "What's Your Legacy?" The campaign is designed to help strengthen marriages in the black community while providing a proud legacy of marriage and family. Nashawn has been featured on the radio and television and has served on various national and military spouse support organizations and churches. Nashawn has been married to Keith for 19 years and they have three children. They live in the Metro DC area.

www.ingramcontent.com/pod-product-compliance
Ingram Content Group UK Ltd.
Pitfield, Milton Keynes, MK11 3LW, UK
UKHW041954230426
12048UKWH00008B/337